"In this bo ... liar, the mirth in the
mundane, t ... ay living."—BOB HOPE

"If Mr. Clean Calls, Tell Him I'm Not In!"

A Funny Look at Family Life

by Bob Hope's comedy writer

Martha Bolton

Regal Books

A Division of GL Publications
Ventura, California, U.S.A.

Published by Regal Books
A Division of GL Publications
Ventura, California 93006
Printed in U.S.A.

Library of Congress Cataloging-in-Publication Data applied for.

1 2 3 4 5 6 7 8 9 10 / 91 90 89

Rights for publishing this book in other languages are contracted by Gospel
Literature International (GLINT) foundation. GLINT also provides technical
help for the adaptation, translation, and publishing of Bible study resources
and books in scores of languages worldwide. For further information, contact
GLINT, Post Office Box 488, Rosemead, California, 91770, U.S.A., or the
publisher.

To my sister Linda
... with love

CONTENTS

FOREWORD

by Bob Phillips
Author of *The World's Greatest Collection of Clean Jokes*

Someone has said, "You know it's going to be a bad day when your twin brother forgets your birthday." I suppose that's better than driving down the freeway behind a group of Hell's Angels when your horn gets stuck.

Martha Bolton takes a tongue-in-cheek look at common pressures like these. She helps us to see that the trouble with life is that it is so *daily*. She helps us to laugh and not cry under stress.

We all have experienced frustrating days and pressured schedules like those Martha writes about. I know I have felt like the Texan who rushed up to the airplane ticket counter and said, "Quick, give me a ticket."

"Where to?" asked the clerk.

"Anywhere," the Texan answered. "I've got business all over."

Martha Bolton knows that the good experiences in life and the not so good experiences happen to all people. Not everyone, however, looks at those events with positive eyes, as the author helps us learn to do.

Too many are like the pessimist who went duck hunting with the optimist. The optimist wanted to show the pessimist his new dog. When the first duck was shot, the optimist sent his dog to fetch the duck. The dog ran across the top of the water and brought back the duck. The pessimist said nothing. A second and third duck hit the lake, and the dog fetched them the same way—by running across the top of the water. Still, the pessimist did not respond. Finally, the optimist couldn't stand it any longer. He said, "Don't you see anything unusual about my new dog?"

"Yes," replied the pessimist, "he can't swim."

Although Martha sees the optimist, humorous side of life, she is not afraid to poke fun at budgets, potlucks and having the minister over for dinner. She is even bold enough to take a humorous look at love and marriage. She would understand times like last week when my wife informed me that our car was flooded. "Where is it?" I asked.

"It's in the backyard in the swimming pool."

"It's flooded, all right," I said.

That doesn't mean that my wife and I don't get along. In fact, we have found the secret of a happy marriage. It's dinner out twice a week by candlelight and soft music. This is followed by a nice, slow walk home. (She eats out on Tuesdays and I eat out on Fridays.)

Martha helps us gain the perspective that God is there and He cares even when it's "One of Those Days." When the tough days come, I think of one of my favorite verses from the Bible. It is found in Luke 2:1: "And it came to pass in those days . . . . " And I'm sure glad it didn't come to stay.

I hope that you will enjoy this book as much as I did. I hope that it will help you to gain a positive perspective. May everyone laugh with you, instead of at you. And remember, you may not always be humorous, but you are funny.

8

ACKNOWLEDGMENTS

I wish to thank:

- My husband, Russ, who has recently developed a real interest in nutrition. Last night he said, "Stay out of the kitchen, dear."

- My sons Rusty, Matt and Tony, who think the family dinner table is the corner booth at Denny's.

- My skilled but gentle editor, Kathi Mills, who never complained about last-minute changes.

- The staff at Regal Books, who've been a pleasure to work with.

- The Millie's Gang (they know who they are) for all the lunches and excuses to procrastinate.

- And finally, to all of you across this great land who know the value of a good joke—but picked up this book anyway. I thank you . . . .

1
IT'S GONNA BE ONE OF THOSE DAYS, LORD

Your dentist informed you that he's got
good news and bad news. The good
news is he can fix your teeth. The bad
news is they won't be in your mouth
when he does it.

Oh, well, things could be worse.
I could have a flat tire.

Have you ever had one of those days when nothing seemed to go right?

—Your alarm clock didn't go off. (Okay, maybe it did go off since it's now in pieces at the foot of your bed, but it didn't wake you up.)

—Breakfast didn't turn out quite the way you expected. (You were hoping you'd only need *one* fire engine to put out the flames.)

—You forgot to pick up your husband's suit at the cleaners and, as luck would have it, none of his ties match his bathrobe.

—You got stuck in an elevator with four insurance salesmen and a guy who just picked up nine rolls of his vacation slides.

—The dog ate your son's science project and is now picking up cable TV. (And they're billing you for it.)

—You ran over something while backing out of your driveway. (Luckily, though, the police officer said he wasn't seriously injured.)

—Your grocery store shopping cart lost a wheel and they had to send for a tow-cart to help you to the check-out counter.

—Your two-year-old decided to change his hairdo—he added his dinner to it.

—That slowpoke you tailgated and honked at for 15 miles turned out to be your pastor.

—You found out your name, address and the precise time you eat dinner was just listed in the National Door-to-Door Salesmen's Directory.

—Your barber let his other customers use your scalp as a mirror.

—Your dentist informed you that he's got good news and bad news. The good news is he can fix your teeth. The bad news is they won't be in your mouth when he does it.

—Your son rode his skateboard across your newly waxed floor four hours ago and still hasn't come in for a landing.

—You pulled a muscle, sprained your wrist and chipped a fingernail trying to twist the safety lid off your bottle of vitamins.

—Your daughter brought home her new boyfriend and he was wearing enough metal to put U.S. Steel out of business.

—Your car got a flat tire while being towed away for engine problems.

—Your beautician made you sign a waiver stating you wouldn't sue if it still looked like you.

—You called home to leave a message but got cut off by your own telephone answering machine.

—Your kid called from college asking for more money. You send it, then realize you don't have a kid.

—For the first time there's only one person in line in front of you at the bank . . . but he's robbing it.

—You broke your ankle in your "Aerobics for Better Health" class.

—Your paper boy threw your paper on a different, less accessible part of the roof.

—You dropped your first aid kit on your foot, then got frostbite from the ice pack you put on it.

—You got a "Let's do lunch!" invitation—from the IRS.

But even on days like this, isn't it nice to know our heavenly Father is with us? He can turn our vexations into victories, our trials into triumphs. We need only to trust Him and remember when things go wrong, He has a way of making everything right again.

2
DIAL-A-PARENT

If they want a raise in their allowance,
they'd be instructed to hang up and
try again later.

Please continue to hold while we on this end of the
line sneak out and go home.

Have you encountered one of those new direct-dialing telephone systems yet? That's where you call a place of business but instead of talking with a live operator, you're instructed to play push buttons with their machine until it eventually transfers your call to the person with whom you wish to speak.

A lot of department stores are using them. After a taped message thanking you for your call, the machine instructs you to press *2* if you want Sporting Goods, *4* if you want Small Appliances, and *9* if you don't really care what department you get, you just like pressing buttons.

Then, once you've coded in your desired department, the machine proceeds to ask more specific questions. If you want to know about a sale item, you're to press *3*; if you have a problem with a product, you need to press *5*; and if you wish to confess pulling the tags off all your mattresses, you'll need to press *7* and throw yourself on the mercy of Beautyrest.

Hospitals have begun using the direct dialing systems, too. If you want the Emergency Room, you dial *1*. Pediatrics? Dial *6*. Dialing *8* gets you Respiratory Therapy, and for Medical Records, you dial *3*. Of course, pitching the telephone against the wall will put your call directly through to the staff psychologist.

I could probably use a direct-dial system on my telephone—you know, for when the kids call. If they want Mom, they'd be instructed to press *8*. If it's Dad they want, they can press *9*. If they're going to be late for dinner, they press *6*. If they need to be picked up, they press *5*. If they want a raise in their allowance, they'd be

19

instructed to hang up and try again later. If they want to borrow the car, they'd be told this number is no longer in service. And if it's report card day, they'd be asked to hold while their call is transferred to Dial-a-Prayer.

Actually, when you think about it, it's really not such a bad idea.

3

HAPPY ARE THE PARENTS WHOSE KIDS ARE AT YOUTH CAMP

I worried my children would have to
sleep in dust-filled cabins and eat lousy
food, and it would feel so much like
home they'd never get homesick.

"But, Mom, youth camp is a month away. Why are you packing now?"

I remember the first time my children went off to youth camp. I worried so much, I couldn't eat. I couldn't sleep. I couldn't get that one question out of my mind: What if they come back early?

Actually, I did worry that weekend. I worried about a lot of things. I worried my children would have to sleep in dust-filled cabins and eat lousy food, and it would feel so much like home they'd never get homesick.

I worried about all the wild animals. What if a bear, snake or coyote happened to wander into a cabin filled with a dozen or so young teenaged boys? Would the poor animal ever be the same again?

I worried about how big the forest was and how easy it would be to become separated from the rest of the group. But everyone assured me the counselors wouldn't get lost.

I prayed that weekend, too.

I prayed the only souvenir my sons would bring home wouldn't be poison ivy. I prayed for our youth pastor who started out on the trip sane. I prayed he'd be able to return to society without an extensive rehabilitation program.

I prayed for our church bus driver that he'd not only have a safe trip up and back, but he'd retain most of his hearing, as well.

I prayed that the boys would be free from harm, have a good time and grow in the Lord.

But most of all, I prayed that their father and I would survive the weekend without them. After all, without any spats to referee, radios to turn down or bathroom mirrors to wait in line in front of, what else would we have to do for fun?

4
I ONLY HAVE EARS FOR YOU
or
THE TELEPHONE AND ME—
A LOVE STORY

There was a day when I could dial out
any time I wanted. I didn't have to take
a number and wait for the receiver to
be surgically removed from
someone's hand.

The famous, "It's for me!" telephone tackle.

I don't think it's right for children to be on the telephone from morning 'til night. That's a mother's job.

All right, I confess, I do enjoy talking on the phone (I once did a book report on the Yellow Pages), but now that my children have started receiving their own calls, I hardly get near the instrument anymore.

Oh, I'm reasonably sure we still have a telephone. Why else would the phone company call me each month and thank me for keeping them in business?

And every once in a while I think I hear it ring. It's either the phone or the smoke alarm telling me dinner's ready.

There was a day when I could dial out anytime I wanted, too. I didn't have to take a number and wait for the receiver to be surgically removed from someone's hand.

I could also talk as long as I liked. I didn't have a teenager at my side bribing me with his month's allowance and, when the time comes, the nursing home of my choice if I'd clear the line.

Isn't it nice, though, that prayer doesn't work that way? We never have to wait for someone else to clear the line so we can talk to God. We can call Him anytime of the day or night and we'll get through. No waiting. No busy signal. No problem.

5
IF GOD GAVE
SPEEDING TICKETS

We eat in a hurry. I'm not saying how
many fast-food restaurants I go to, but
the other day I caught myself ordering
into my mailbox and driving around
the house.

"It sounds good, but who's got the time to wait?"

Have you ever found yourself wishing your microwave would hurry up?

Do you get impatient mixing your instant coffee?

The last time you stopped and smelled the roses, were they in a can of Glade?

Is your appointment calendar booked up into the after-life?

Is your panting keeping the dog awake?

Have you ever thought of renting the space shuttle just so you can get all your errands done?

If you answered "yes" to any of the above (personally, I scored a five-out-of-six), then perhaps it's time to slow down on life's road and enjoy the trip a bit more.

Slowing down isn't easy, though. Life today seems permanently set in high gear. From the moment we wake up in the morning, we're driving the fast lane with no speed bumps in sight.

We eat in a hurry. I'm not saying how many fast-food restaurants I go to, but the other day I caught myself ordering into my mailbox and driving around the house.

We work in a hurry. We've got computers, FAX machines, call-waiting, beepers—and that's just for our preschoolers.

Our driving has speeded up, too. I'm amazed at how fast some people drive these days. No wonder you see signs that say "Speed checked by aircraft." It's the only way anyone can catch up to them.

At times, praying even gets rushed. We may get in such a hurry that we bow our heads and bring them up so fast we get whiplash.

31

We're in the age of instant breakfasts, 60-second hair conditioners and drive-through surgical centers. We get our clothes cleaned in an hour and our printing done while we wait. We want it today, not tomorrow; this second, not this afternoon.

But why all the rush? Why not take a moment to let the coffee percolate? Why not tap the brakes a little and reevaluate what's really important in life?

Our only free day shouldn't be February 29 every other leap year, and our only stroll down the boulevard shouldn't be when we run out of gas. After all, the world God created isn't spinning any faster. So, why should His children?

6
THE FAMILY VACATION
or
FIFTY WAYS TO ANSWER
"ARE WE THERE YET?"

By the time a family vacation is over,
we ... have grown a little closer. My
husband and I can truthfully say we've
opened up more to the children—his
wallet, my purse, our credit card holder.

"Thank goodness this is only an overnighter!"

Each year you know it's coming. You try to prepare for it. You try to brace yourself for it. But no matter what you do, it seems you're never quite ready for . . . the family vacation.

Family vacations, though, do have their plus side. They give you time to get to know one another again, time to communicate. I know whenever our family goes on a vacation, the communication begins the moment we pull out of the driveway. My husband is usually the first to open up.

"Uh, dear," he'll begin, "why are we towing a six-foot U-Haul trailer full of suitcases when we're only going to be staying *four* days?"

"You're absolutely right, dear. I really should have rented the truck."

"But the only things you left behind were the carpets."

"That's not true," I'll answer. "What do you think I used for padding?"

The communication takes a different turn a few minutes down the road.

"Sweetheart," he says with a smile, "did you remember to turn off the sprinklers?"

"You never told me to turn off the sprinklers."

"Well, did you check to see if all the burners were turned off?"

"No, but don't worry. If the house catches on fire, the sprinklers will put it out."

For some reason that's never a good enough answer, and inevitably he'll announce, "I'm turning around. We're going back to check."

"Going back?" the kids grumble from the rear seat.

"But, Dad, the neighbors will call the fire department if they see smoke coming out of our windows."

"Not necessarily. They'll probably just think your mother's cooking again."

And so, we go back. We always go back. In fact, my youngest son once wrote a school paper on "How I Spent My Summer Vacation Making U-Turns in Front of My House.

After a quick recheck of the homestead, we'll continue on our trip and the communication resumes. It's the children's turn now to share their innermost feelings.

"Aren't we there yet?"

"Well then, when are we going to get there?"

"He's kicking me!"

"Am not!"

"Are too!"

"Dad, what does it mean when a policeman turns his red lights on behind you?"

This openness usually continues throughout the remainder of the trip.

"How come he always gets to sit by the window?"

"Can you turn the radio up louder? I still have some of my hearing left."

"What do you mean, the Grand Canyon doesn't have rides?"

Amazingly enough, though, by the time a family vacation is over, we really have grown a little closer. My husband and I can truthfully say we've opened up more to the children—his wallet, my purse, our credit card holder. And the children haven't held back sharing their aspirations, their goals—like, "Can we go home now?"

So, you see, a family vacation can be a wonderful thing. Just make sure you schedule a second vacation to rest up from it.

7

THE BACKSEAT DRIVER'S HALL OF FAME

Why is he always saying that when he goes to the funny farm, I'll be the one driving him there?

"Uh, dear . . . do you think you could hit those speed
bumps just a little easier?"

If ever there's a backseat driver's Hall of Fame, I'll no doubt be the first inductee. I take my backseat driving seriously. I tell my husband when he needs to drive faster, drive slower, turn right, turn left, make a U-turn or park. And he appreciates it. After all, he knows I'm better behind the wheel than he is. Why else is he always saying that when he goes to the funny farm, I'll be the one driving him there?

When you get right down to it, though, men are far worse backseat drivers than women. My husband continually criticizes me for my three-point turns. He doesn't think two of the points should involve tow trucks. He never seems satisfied with the way I park, either. For some reason, he's of the opinion our car should retain some of its paint when I do it. And I don't know why, but my husband is always nagging at me not to stop on railroad tracks. Doesn't he realize that, with that train coming, I can't hear him anyway?

Still, no matter how well intentioned backseat driving is, it's probably best to leave the decisions to the person who has the keenest perspective of the situation—the person behind the wheel. The person in control.

This is true of life, also. Sometimes we may find ourselves trying to backseat drive with God. We tell Him when we think His answer is too slow. We wonder why He's chosen this route instead of that one. Or we try to find our own shortcuts, only to have them turn into dead ends.

How much better would it be if we merely placed our trust in His judgment? After all, who better to have sitting behind the wheel guiding our lives than the One who knows the road better than any of us? In other words, maybe we need to relax a little more and leave the driving to Him.

8
THE FAMILY BUDGET AND OTHER GREAT SOURCES OF HUMOR

Nowadays, when you ring for a butcher, it's not to cut your meat. It's for a loan application.

"With all the bills we get, we had to let it go condo!"

Every family ought to have a budget—a list that shows exactly what you'll need to borrow from American Express to pay off your VISA card so you can use it to charge your MasterCard payment so you'll be below your limit and can use that to charge your Discovery and Diner's Club payments.

A family budget, however, isn't the easiest thing to agree upon. Whenever my husband and I try to make one out, he will inevitably propose all the cutbacks in my spending alone. He will make ridiculous demands like, "Don't buy so much from the Avon lady that she has to airlift your order to our porch." He will insist I throw away my I.D. bracelet that says, "If found, please return me to the nearest mall." He will even recommend the phone company come out and disconnect my private line to Teleshopper.

Eventually, though, we do come to a compromise on what the spending cuts should be, and for the most part, we try to adhere to them. These days you have to. The cost of living is too high not to budget your money.

For one thing, the price of food has skyrocketed. Nowadays, when you ring for a butcher, it's not to cut your meat. It's for a loan application.

Clothing costs have risen dramatically, too. I can remember a time when house dresses didn't come with a mortgage, and buying a business suit didn't mean you had to sell the business.

And have you looked at the cost of housing lately? Sure, a man's home is his castle, but should the king and queen have to get second jobs just to pay for it?

Still, even with the mounting prices and tightened budgets, isn't it nice to relax in the knowledge that if we trust in the Lord, He will meet our every need? And He doesn't even charge interest.

9
THE THERMOSTAT WARS
or
MY LOVE IS LIKE A RED, RED NOSE

When he opens the windows, I turn up the heat. When he turns on the air conditioner, I light all the burners on the kitchen stove.

"When I pledged to thee all my worldly goods, I didn't
know it meant all the covers, too!"

When my husband stopped our wedding ceremony to adjust the chapel thermostat, I should have known then what kind of life I was destined to lead with him—especially since I had already adjusted it to my liking on my way down the aisle.

Frankly, I think engaged couples should be given a climatic-compatibility test before taking that big plunge into matrimony.

Over the past 19 years of marriage, I don't think my husband and I have ever agreed on what temperature to keep the house. He prefers it on the cooler side—meaning I can make block ice in my kitchen sink. I, on the other hand, prefer life in a warmer environment. I visit Death Valley only when I want to cool off.

With a determined effort on both our parts, however, we have managed to find several ways to compromise. When he opens the windows, I turn up the heat. When he turns on the air conditioner, I light all the burners on the kitchen stove. And when he sets his side of the electric blanket to "Night of the Glacier," I know that's my cue to turn my side up to a more suitable setting (somewhere between "The San Francisco Fire" and "Evening at Three Mile Island").

Another way we've found to compromise is for me to dress warmer around the house—you know, ski jacket, fur-lined boots, lead apron. This works out all right, but it tends to get a little heavy in the shower.

That compromise is the key to a happy marriage is something I've come to realize. It doesn't matter if he has the house so cold I can make ice sculptures out of my

47

breath, or if I've got it so hot even the dog's trying to take off its coat. All that matters is being together. And my husband agrees. It really does go back to our wedding day. When it came time to lift the veil, I told him to put it back down; he was letting in a draft. He should have known then what he was in for.

10
NO LUCK WITH POTLUCKS
or
TAKE MY DISH—PLEASE!

Most of my cooking leaves something to
be desired (namely, a stomach pump
and notification of the partaker's
next of kin).

"I think I know which dish is Mom's"

Which dish is yours, Mom?"

Now, there's a question my children have never asked at a church potluck. They know exactly which dish is mine. That's because they have been briefed ahead of time and have received their instructions.

You see, the rule of our house is that each family member is to spot my dish on the serving table and take a minimum of two scoops. Any brave family member willing to go the extra mile and take three scoops gets an additional hour on their play time and first dibs on the Pepto-Bismol.

All of this is necessary, of course, to make sure the dish I've slaved over, the dish I've worked all night on, the dish I've proudly prepared, doesn't—as in years past—get mistaken for the scraps bowl.

Now, I'll admit, most of my cooking leaves something to be desired (namely, a stomach pump and notification of the partaker's next of kin), but it still hurts to watch church member after church member walk past my culinary masterpiece without slowing down a beat. In fact, some of the flies even seem to take the long way around just to avoid it.

I've often wished I could cook like those women whose dishes disappear two minutes after they set them out. It never fails that hungry attendees will be scraping the bottom of their pans while my casserole just sits there and spoils.

In fact, in all the years I've been potlucking, I can recall only one time when my dish disappeared quickly. But, unfortunately, no one's needed a door stop since.

I suppose when you get right down to it, I can't really

blame the folks for passing on my cooking. It's just that when they do, I have to take it back home with me, which creates another problem:

Do you have any idea how much crane companies charge these days?

11
COMPUTER BILLING THAT BYTES
or
IF YOU'VE ALREADY MAILED YOUR PAYMENT, DON'T THINK *WE'RE* GONNA BELIEVE YOU!

Your credit privileges have been revoked, and our representatives have all been issued your picture and the names of your family members.

"Are you who I should see about my bill?"

If you've ever had a disagreement with a computer over the slightest billing error, you know the battle usually goes something like this:

Computer, letter dated October 30
Dear Valued Customer:

We hate to mention this, but as of this date we have not received your payment. Won't you kindly send your remittance at your earliest convenience?

Again, we are sorry to bother you. We trust you will take this letter in the tone it was intended.

Thank you, and have a nice day.

Customer, letter dated November 6
Dear Sir:

I mailed my payment for $35 on October 1. A copy of the cancelled check is enclosed. Kindly adjust your records accordingly.

Thank you.

Computer, letter dated November 20, stamped:
URGENT—READ AT ONCE
Dear Mrs. Past-Due:

Credit is a valuable thing. Most people want to do everything they can to protect their good credit. So, why don't you?

Since you have ignored our first letter and have not sent in your payment, your credit privileges are now in jeopardy.

Won't you please get with it and send in your check for $35 today?

Thank you, and have a nice day.

Customer, letter dated November 26
Dear Sir:

Don't you read your mail? I sent you my check #543 on October 1. I also sent you a copy of my cancelled check cashed by you on October 8.

I am now enclosing another copy for your reference, and I would appreciate your immediate crediting of my account.

Thank you.

Computer, letter dated December 4, written in red ink
DEAR MADAM:

SINCE YOU HAVE CONTINUED TO IGNORE OUR PREVIOUS REQUESTS FOR PAYMENT, YOU LEAVE US NO ALTERNATIVE OTHER THAN TO TAKE FURTHER ACTION TO PROTECT OUR INTERESTS.

WE FEEL WE HAVE GIVEN YOU AMPLE OPPORTUNITY TO MAKE GOOD YOUR DELINQUENCY. BUT YOU HAVE MADE NO EFFORT WHATSOEVER TO COMMUNICATE WITH US. IT'S CLODS LIKE YOU WITH OUTSTANDING DEBTS WHO DRIVE THE COST OF LIVING OUT OF SIGHT. HOW DID WE EVER GIVE YOU CREDIT IN THE FIRST PLACE?

YOUR CLEAN RECORD AND GOOD CREDIT RATING MAY HAVE FOOLED US AT FIRST, BUT NOW WE'VE GOT YOUR NUMBER, YOU FLAKE! AND YOU CAN REST ASSURED WE'RE GOING TO INFORM ALL THE CREDIT BUREAUS ABOUT THIS SO YOU CAN'T PULL YOUR LITTLE SCHEME ON ANYBODY ELSE.

However, since you have been a good customer in the past, we're going to give you until December 5 to send us your check, which, by the time you receive this, was probably yesterday.

We hope you take this letter in the tone it was intended. Thank you, and have a nice day.

Customer, letter dated December 9
Dear Sir:

Now you're beginning to get on my nerves. I have paid the bill in question. I have sent you two copies of the cancelled check. A third one is enclosed.

So, please, quit sending me bills!

Computer Mailgram, dated December 20
Dear Parasite:

Because of your good record, we have tried to be lenient. We have tried to be fair. But we don't even like you anymore.

You continue to ignore our letters, and now we have no choice. Your credit privileges have been revoked, and our representatives have all been issued your picture and the names of your family members.

The next correspondence you receive will be from our collection agency.

Watch for it . . . and have a nice day.

Collection agency jerk-gram, dated December 25
Merry Christmas!

Allow us to introduce ourselves. We are a collection agency. We make our living collecting from jerks like you.

You have until midnight tonight to deck our halls with your payment, or we deck you.

Do we make ourselves clear?

Thank you, and have a nice day.

Customer telegram, dated December 25

Dear Sir:

I don't believe this. I've paid you, you've cashed my check, I've sent you three copies of the cancelled check, but you continue to ignore my letters.

Now it's fight-back time. I'm calling in Ralph Nader, the Better Business Bureau and Mike Wallace. When they get through with you, you'll be sorry.

Computer, letter dated January 3

Dear Valued Customer:

Thank you for your payment.

Your credit has been reinstated and, as one of our valued customers, we are happy to inform you that your credit line has been increased.

Why put off all those things you've been wanting to buy? Come in today and just say, "Charge it." We'll bill you later. It's as simple as that.

So remember, just say, "Charge it" and your worries are over.

Thank you, and do have a nice day.

All I can say is, aren't you glad our prayers to God aren't handled by a computer?

12
HAVING FAITH FOR THE IMPOSSIBLE
or
THE PAPER-BAG SCHOOL OF BEAUTY

If I smiled my cheeks would crack and
my forehead would crumble into my
lap, but I was a new person.

"But this is the 'new' me. The old me made the
appointment. Bill her!"

I've never considered myself photogenic. Oh, I take a nice picture every once in a while—when the lens cap is left on. And I look great in group shots. (Hands Across America was my best one yet.) But close-up pictures of me generally leave a lot to be desired—like distance.

So, you can well imagine my excitement when I discovered a photographer who would not only take my portrait, but would first give me a complete make-over. Considering his special make-up, hairstyling and lighting, I figured I had to come away with at least one good shot.

With visions of a poster-worthy finished product, I excitedly made an appointment. Creating a new me, however, wasn't going to be easy. On the morning of my photo session, I awoke with so many pillow creases on my face I couldn't tell if I was looking at my cheeks or a map of the California fault system. And there were enough bags under my eyes to put Hefty out of business. Still, I kept the faith and went.

The make-over began with a camouflaging foundation. This was to hide any blemishes, liver spots or skin discolorations I might have. They applied it with a spray gun.

Next came the challenge of finding a base makeup closest to my natural skin color, which ended up being a cross between "Clown White" and "Anemic Glory."

Now, it was time to add some color to my cheeks. After debating between a soft rose, a deep pink and a blood transfusion, he made the decision to go with the rose.

With eye shadows, mascara and eyeliner, he was able to make my eyes look bigger and brighter, and he also managed to accomplish something I've never been able to do before. He made them look like a matched set.

With a special lip brush, he redefined my lips, giving them the more traditional horizontal look.

It was time now for my hair. He fluffed it up, pulled it over, teased it mercilessly and basically gave it a fullness even Don King doesn't enjoy.

After approximately an hour and a half (he didn't even charge extra for overtime), I was a new person. I looked 15 years younger. The bags had disappeared, the fault lines were gone. I looked healthy, vibrant. The transformation was amazing. Of course, if I smiled my cheeks would crack and my forehead would crumble into my lap, but I was a new person.

All in all, it was a fun day, but the best part was when I was able to get home and comb out my hair, chisel off my makeup and get back to being myself again. Being very nearly glamorous was nice, but what's nicer is knowing God loves me just the way I am.

13

THE FAMILY THAT WHEEZES TOGETHER . . .

We've organized a few family baseball games, but they never let me play my favorite position—fan.

"Mom's doing much better with her exercise program, don't you agree?"

I believe it's a good idea for families to exercise together. That way, when Mom collapses, there'll be someone there to call the paramedics.

My family and I have tried several means of group exercise. We've gone through obstacle courses together. (It's the only way to get from one end of our house to the other.)

Family basketball games are fun, too, although I usually get called for traveling. Not the regular kind of traveling, mind you. They just catch me trying to sneak off to the snack bar.

We've also organized a few family baseball games, but they never let me play my favorite position—fan.

Exhilarating, challenging, push-to-the-limit sort of hikes are something we try to do on a regular basis. They're beginning to get too rough for me, though. Lately, everyone's been wanting to go beyond our driveway.

We've even joined a health club together. There, Dad spends his time lifting weights, the kids will usually opt for racquetball and I'll try to swim at least four laps a visit. I could probably do more laps, but it's not that easy to turn around in a Jacuzzi.

Yet, with all the importance of getting physical exercise together, it's even more important for a family to exercise its spiritual muscles together. Reading the Bible and praying as a unit builds spiritual endurance and strength. And staying in shape in that department is one of the best things a family can do.

14
IF MR. CLEAN CALLS, TELL HIM I'M NOT IN!

When my Airwick Solid melts 15 minutes after I set it out, I figure it's probably trying to tell me something.

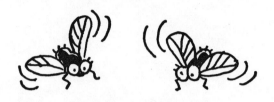

"Quick! The front door's open. Let's make a run for it!"

I hate housework. I only do it when it's absolutely necessary—like when I can't find one of the kids. Or when the floral pattern on my bedsheets starts taking root.

There are other signs I watch for that let me know it's time to clean the house. For instance, when I find snow at the top of my dirty clothes pile, I know washday is at hand. Or when a rude guest signs in on my coffee table with her fingers, I concede it might be time to drag out the Pledge. And when my Airwick Solid melts 15 minutes after I set it out, I figure it's probably trying to tell me something.

Yet, even though I'm the only woman in the world who owns a washing machine with a mildew cycle, I still realize housekeeping is a necessary part of life. Boarding up the shower is no way to get rid of unsightly lime stains, and the dishwasher overflowing shouldn't be a prerequisite to mopping the kitchen floor.

It's just that I don't want to overdo it. You know, like those people whose houses smell of so much Lysol, every time you take a breath you disinfect your lungs. These people are so clean and tidy, you couldn't have archeological digs on their dresser tops. They'd never have so many dishes on their kitchen sink they forget what color it is. And pest exterminators would never consider using their homes for training maneuvers.

But I prefer to think the perfect housekeeper is someone who can strike a happy medium. It's like the old saying, "A home should be clean enough to be healthy, but dirty enough to be happy."

Or to put it another way, "Keep your floors clean enough to eat off of, but leave enough food there to make it worth your while!"

15

I DON'T CARE IF IT IS COOL. YOU ARE *NOT* SHAMPOOING YOUR HAIR WITH THE EASTER EGG DYE!

How can we know if our children's hair is rainbow colors intentionally or if it's from a severe vitamin deficiency requiring medical attention?

"Sure, we could fade them, rip out the knees, and make
them look more worn, but it'll cost extra."

I think someone should come out with a "Parent's Guide to Cool." It would be sort of a reference tool that parents could refer to when trying to decide whether their off-spring are merely dressing with the times or whether something did, in fact, explode in their closet.

Parents should not be expected to keep up with what's in and what's out, what's chic and what's geek. How can we know if our children's hair is rainbow colors intentionally or if it's from a severe vitamin deficiency requiring medical attention? How are we supposed to know if jeans with ripped knees are in style or merely the result of a moth on a high-fiber denim diet?

Naturally, the guidebook would need to be updated on a regular basis. Fads change quickly. The other day I bought an outfit that went out of style before the clerk could put it into the bag.

It might also be helpful if the guidebook included a Dictionary of Cool Talk. This is so we'll be able to understand what language it is that they're speaking instead of automatically assuming too much mousse has seeped in through their scalp and is now affecting their brain.

There is a market for such a book, but until someone sees fit to publish it, I guess parents are on their own.

To be perfectly honest, though, I haven't really minded the wrinkled look, the torn look, or even the faded look. After all, I haven't had to say, "Why don't you take better care of your clothes?" for years.

16
THE PASTOR'S VISIT
or
NOW, WHERE DID I PUT THAT BIBLE?

My family loves it when I invite a man
of the cloth for dinner. They're for
anyone who will help them pray
over my cooking.

"I see the pastor's coming over for dinner again."

Through the years, I've entertained many pastors in my home. In fact, my family loves it when I invite a man of the cloth for dinner. They're for anyone who will help them pray over my cooking.

But for some of us, having the pastor over for dinner requires a little extra preparation. For one thing, we have to make sure the church bulletin is put away—you know, the one with all the doodling on it. We wouldn't want him to think we weren't paying attention in church last Sunday.

Of course, we need to take down our appointment calendar from the kitchen wall, too. After we've been telling him how we're too busy to help in the church, it would be a shame for him to see how many free days we really do have.

Camouflaging that new boat in our driveway so it will blend in with the shrubbery wouldn't be a bad idea, either—especially since last week was Pledge Sunday and we made that big speech about how we would give if only we could.

Provided there's time, adding a few Sunday School quarterlies and devotionals to the living room decor is always a nice touch. Preferably, they should be open to the chapter we would have been studying if only we had the time to be studying it.

Finally, we need to forewarn the children that when grace is said, it might last a little longer than usual. That's so they won't act surprised and say something embarrassing like, "Boy, what happened to, 'The turkey's carved. Thanks, Lord, I'm starved!'"

Going to all this trouble to impress a member of the

clergy is fine, but we shouldn't forget an even more important Guest. This Guest is at our table for every meal and in our home every day. Maybe we should be giving as much thought to the kind of impression we're making on Him.

17

THE FAMILY CAMP-OUT
or
WHAT DO YOU MEAN, PIZZA-MAN DOESN'T DELIVER OUT HERE?

Since we had pitched our tent in the dark, we unknowingly set it on top of an automatic sprinkler, and it was just a matter of time before we'd all have to get up anyway.

"It's a beautiful campsite, dear, but where do I plug in
the microwave?"

I suppose I should have known, when my husband bought camping equipment several years ago, he'd expect me to escape with him every once in a while to the great out-doors.

But I'm not the camping type. I'll go camping when Coleman makes a microwave and tents start coming with "Best Western" signs. You see, taking a shower under a two-foot faucet and spraying insect repellent on so thick I gain four pounds is not my idea of a vacation. I don't like dirt in my food, bugs in my drink or rocks in my bed. If I wanted all that, I'd just stay home. I don't like the crowds either. I'm not into elbow-to-elbow fishing, mob hiking, or taking in the scenic view of 400 R.V. vehicles. Nor do I enjoy using barbecue pits on the time-share program.

Still, every so often I lose the family-vacation vote and have to go.

Take, for instance, last summer. I cast my vote for Hawaii. My husband (and savings account) voted for a week of camping. The kids voted for camping, too, citing how much they enjoyed watching me cook over a blazing fire. I reminded them that was how I cooked all our meals, (around our house "variable low cloudiness" has come to mean "soup's on") but it was no use. Before I knew it, we were pulling into a campground my husband had seen advertised in *Mosquito Travel* magazine.

"This is it?" I grumbled, surveying the tumbleweeds.

"Isn't it great?" my husband exclaimed, taking in the view from the highest point of the camp—an anthill.

"This is it?" I repeated.

He nodded proudly.

81

"But isn't that a chemical dump site over there on the other side of that fence?" I asked, pointing off in the distance.

Pretending he didn't hear me, he mumbled something about it getting dark, then asked me to assist him with our new "easy set-up" tent.

Now, setting up an "easy set-up" tent requires only three things: skill, patience and the telephone number of a nearby Ramada Inn, just in case.

You may not realize it, but the words "easy set-up" are merely code words for "You ain't ever gonna get this together, brother!" In fact, that's why they always include a picture of the tent along with the directions. It's so you can see what the tent would have looked like had you not given up on it and thrown it into the lake.

After four hours of "easy set-up," my husband finally finished our canvas abode. It leaned eight different directions (none of them upright). And that wasn't the only problem. We couldn't zip the door shut either. Every time we tried the window would fly open. Then, if we managed to shut both the door and the window, the roof would collapse.

Too tired to battle it any longer, we decided to leave well enough alone and sleep with the door open. If a wild animal happened to wander in during the night, all I knew was he wasn't getting my pillow.

Before long, everyone was asleep. Everyone but me, that is. I couldn't get to sleep because of all the night sounds—you know, crickets, owls, the rock band practicing in the next tent over. (I'm not saying how loud it was, but when was the last time you saw squirrels stuffing nuts in their ears?)

It didn't really matter, though, because, since we had pitched our tent in the dark, we unknowingly set it on top of an automatic sprinkler, and it was just a matter of time before we'd all have to get up anyway.

Morning found me dressed and ready to start cooking breakfast. They say there's nothing quite like waking up to the aroma of bacon sizzling over an open fire, so I quickly woke up my family so they could enjoy it coming from the other camp sites before I started cooking.

There was, though, a positive side to my camp fire delicacies. While all the other campers had to put up with hundreds of bees buzzing around their food, my food drew only the ones with nothing to live for.

Still, all in all, the week wasn't that bad. We got to tell stories around the camp fire, go for long hikes and basically enjoy each other away from the fast pace of big city life. And even though I had so many bites, I felt like a club med for mosquitos, I realize it's important to get away from it all every once in a while, to rough it, to go without modern conveniences.

And, yes, I have to admit, I'd do it all over again—but next time, I'm holding out for a camp ground with valet parking and room service.

18

SOME ASSEMBLY REQUIRED
or
WHY DAD SPENT TWO MONTHS IN THE GARAGE TALKING TO HIS SOCKET SET

We labored. We sweated. We worked into the night. Finally, we got the box open.

"You're right. We *did* miss a step. The step that said
we should have bought it already assembled."

I remember the Christmas my husband and I bought a new bicycle for one of our boys. Our son was thrilled, excited, elated. But then, right in the midst of all the merriment, something happened to ruin the moment. He asked us to put it together.

I tried to get him just to play with the parts for a month or so, but he wasn't interested. I ripped the picture of the bike off the carton and told him to straddle that for a while. He merely shook his head. He wanted the bike itself, the real thing. And he wanted it to look like the photo.

So, my husband grabbed his tool box, I grabbed an aspirin and we began. We labored. We sweated. We worked into the night. Finally, we got the box open. Then came the real fun—that of trying to decipher the instructions that were written in a hardback trilogy and had more steps than the Taj Mahal.

They did promise, though, that the only tools we would need would be a screwdriver, a hammer and an adjustable wrench. But, by the time we were done, we had used every tool in the garage *except* the screwdriver, hammer and adjustable wrench. (Although, at times, several uses for the hammer did cross our minds.)

After six hours of trying to get *A* into *B*, connect *D* to *F*, slide *G* through *H* while bypassing *E* altogether until Step #9 (at which point we were to overlap *H* with *I*), we finally completed our project. The handlebars were on sideways, the kickstand kicked back and there were six screws unaccounted for, but we were done.

"But it doesn't look anything like the picture," my son moaned.

"Sure, it does," I assured him. Then, snatching the picture from his hands, I cut it into tiny pieces, scrambled them to match up with the contraption we had just built and smiled confidently. "See, now it looks *exactly* like the picture."

"Maybe we should take it back to the store and get some help," my son pleaded. "You know, from the people who made the bike in the first place. They'll know how to put it together."

I had to agree. I'm sure the guy who designed the bike didn't mean for both wheels to be on the same side or the seat to be pointing heavenward.

So we took the bike back to the store and, within minutes, they had it looking and operating precisely as it was meant to. It was beautiful. Our son was thrilled, and my husband and I were in awe of how simple a task it was for someone who knew what he was doing. After all, who better to put a bike together than its maker?

Sometimes we may need a little help assembling our lives, too. No matter how hard we try, we just can't seem to make *A* fit into *B*. We work at it and work at it, but it doesn't end up looking anything like it was supposed to. That's when it's time to gather up all the pieces and take them to the Lord. After all, who better to put a life together than its Maker?

19
FORGET AL CAPONE'S VAULT—FOR REAL ADVENTURE, LET GERALDO OPEN MY CLOSETS!

I usually hit the closets next, leaving a
trail, of course, in case I can't find
my way back out.

"Don't you think it's about time you cleaned out from
under your bed?"

Every once in a while (in a moment of delirium), I decide it's time to clear out the clutters in my home—not just move them from one end of the house to the other, mind you. I mean, really clear them out.

I begin by giving away those stacks and stacks of magazines I haven't gotten around to reading yet—you know, the ones I ordered thinking I'd win my name on a check for ten million dollars, but all I got my name on was a mailing list.

Next, it's my old clothes that go. The basic rule of thumb here is, if the moths have been seen in it more than I have, it gets the heave.

Old toys and worn-out games aren't safe from my anti-clutter mood, either. After all, what good is a Monopoly game if all the properties are on the verge of being condemned?

I usually hit the closets next, leaving a trail, of course, in case I can't find my way back out. When I go into the kids' closets, I leave a will, as well.

The final clutter haven I tackle is under the beds. I'm not saying what excitement that task holds in store for me, but two episodes of "Wild Animal Kingdom" were filmed under there.

But once all the work is done and the clutters have been cleared away, the house does seem a little fresher, a little cleaner, a little more liveable.

From time to time, we may notice our lives becoming cluttered, too. We find ourselves hanging on to things we should have tossed out years ago. We've got this shoved in that corner, that shoved in this corner and this tucked away down here. It's then that we probably need to stop and clear out just a little more room for the Lord.

91

20
DINNER'S READY
or
WHERE ARE YOU GUYS HIDING NOW?

The family dinner table is more than a
testing ground for Rolaids.

"It's time for all your holiday cooking again, eh, lady?"

It's important for families to eat together. That's why I've instructed my children that they are in no way to grab a microwave pizza from the freezer or make themselves a bologna sandwich just before dinner time. After all, if their father and I have to sit down to a home-cooked meal, why shouldn't they?

Besides, the family dinner table is more than a testing ground for Rolaids. It's a place where families can discuss the day's events.

"Your teacher called this afternoon. She said you haven't disrupted the class all week."

"See, I told you I've been trying to behave."

"I know. And being absent all week didn't hurt, either."

Dad's work is discussed next.

"I think the boss is really impressed with me."

"Really? What makes you say that, dear?"

"Well, why else would he call me in today and tell me they couldn't pay him to keep me on."

My day is discussed, too.

"You won't believe who I ran into today."

"And old friend?"

"No. A new Toyota."

But eating together renders something even more important than conversation. It gives a feeling of closeness, a sense of "family."

When it's just the family, we don't have to go into the garage and bring out that extra stool or drag over the piano bench for someone to sit on. There's already a chair reserved for each member. There's a place set for us. We belong.

It's the same in the family of God. We don't have to eat from TV trays or stand off in the corner. There's a chair already reserved for us at His table. There's a place set just for us. We belong.

21
FROM "ENDLESS LOVE" TO "ROMANCING THE STONE"

When my husband and I first met, my
heart fluttered. His heart fluttered. Now,
when our hearts flutter, we just
take an antacid.

"It's a bunion file. Happy Anniversary, dear!"

I'll never forget the year my husband gave car mats to me for our anniversary. And as if that wasn't breathtaking enough, he later took me to a very classy restaurant for dinner—you know, one of those places where you're not allowed to honk in their drive-through lane. That was the same year I wrapped up a Weedwhacker and a bunion file for his gifts.

And who says romance is dead?

Recently, though, we've come to realize you've got to work at keeping a marriage fresh and exciting. If the only reason you dim the lights is to get the glare off the television screen, and the only cuddling you're doing is when the heater breaks down in your car, then perhaps it's time to work a little harder at maintaining that "first-love" relationship.

When my husband and I first met, my heart fluttered. His heart fluttered. Now when our hearts flutter, we just take an antacid.

Back then, we made sure we looked our best for each other, too. He had to have every hair in place and I had to look as though I had just stepped off the cover of *Vogue* magazine (or at least the first couple of pages).

After a few comfortable years of marriage, however, all that's changed. Oh, he still keeps every hair in place, but it really doesn't take that much time to mousse the two of them. And these days, I look more like I stepped off the cover of *Bathrobes Quarterly*.

That's why we agreed to start giving our marriage the attention it deserves. We're doing things to nurture it, pamper it and ensure its longevity.

99

For one thing, we're spending more evenings in front of a warm, crackling fire—only now it's in the fireplace, not in the kitchen. I don't let little things bother me anymore, either—like snoring. I just bought some earplugs and now my husband says he can't even hear me.

You see, we realize that for a marriage to stay healthy it has to be watered, pruned and cared for.

Sometimes, we fall short of giving our relationship with the Lord the attention it deserves, too. As in a marriage, it's easy to begin taking His love for granted, to become complacent in our walk with Him. And, just as in a marriage, we may need to stop from time to time and get back into that first-love relationship with Him.

22
ARE YOU *SURE* THE WISE MEN WORE TURTLENECKS?

The wise men's robes turned out
exceptionally nice—once I remembered
to put in the holes for their heads
to go through.

" . . . and then after the play, we can use it
as a piano cover."

I remember the year my pastor put me in charge of making the costumes for the Christmas pageant. He and the church board felt I was the perfect person for the job. In other words, I wasn't at the planning meeting.

Now, I'll be the first to admit that sewing has never been one of my talents. The blouse that I made in high school is still on display there showing how *not* to sew on sleeves. (Evidently, there's some unwritten rule about attaching only two.)

But not wanting to disappoint the cast, I agreed to give it my best shot.

I finished the shepherd costumes first and, except for the one with the turtleneck and fringe, they turned out rather authentic looking.

To my astonishment, I succeeded with the angel costumes, as well. A few of them had a little more material than they needed (they could have been an ark cover for Noah), but they worked out fine for the play.

Herod's costume was a cinch, although while pinning it on, I stuck the poor actor so many times he should have been awarded a purple heart.

The wise men's robes turned out exceptionally nice also—once I remembered to put in the holes for their heads to go through.

Finally, all the costumes were sewn, the cast looked terrific and I couldn't have been prouder as I sat in the audience that night enjoying the pageant just like every other parent—with an instamatic, a Polaroid, and a video camera.

I learned a valuable lesson that evening, too. Besides

remembering to bring plenty of film, I learned that when the Lord gives us something to do, we should do it. Even when we don't feel qualified for the job, if we'll only trust Him, He will make it work out just fine.

As a matter of fact, I've already volunteered to sew the new choir robes for our church. And as soon as the pastor quits changing his phone number, I can get the go-ahead to start.

23

OF COURSE, COMPANY'S COMING. YOU THINK I'D PUT OUT CLEAN PLATES FOR JUST ANYBODY?

My fine crystal is in boxes shoved in a cupboard while we drink out of souvenir Slurpee cups from 7-11.

"See, we are too having company. Mom put out the
good paper plates!"

Not long ago, it became necessary to replace our old dining room set. It was beginning to sag in the middle (from years of holding up my biscuits, no doubt), and it bore numerous knife marks and scratches (from dinner guests who had opted for the easier task of cutting through it instead of my meatloaf).

In its place we bought a new French provincial dining table along with six chairs, two leaves and a shine you could tan by. It was beautiful. Day after day, week after week, I'd walk past it admiringly. My husband would comment on how nice it looked. My children were even impressed.

Then, the inevitable came. One day, my eldest son asked if we were ever planning to eat off it or were we merely saving it for a souvenir.

He had a point.

I don't know why it is, but too often we tend to save our best and newest things for company.

My good china is in my buffet collecting dust while the family and I eat off designer Dixieware.

My fine crystal is in boxes shoved in a cupboard while we drink out of souvenir Slurpee cups from 7-11.

I even have brand new bed sheets that I've been saving for guests. Meanwhile, my husband and I get the ones that only fit when I roll up our mattress like a croissant.

But my son's comment that day reminded me it doesn't have to be like that. After all, what dinner guests could be more important to me than my own family?

So, right then and there, I determined things were going to be different. I was going to treat my family to a

107

very special "company" type meal (you know, where you use forks).

This time, when my son walked by the table, he looked at his crystal-clear reflection in the china, which I had meticulously placed around the table, and naturally inquired, "How does my hair look?"

Then he went on to ask, "Someone special coming for dinner tonight, Mom?"

I nodded.

"You're looking at him."

24

PARENTS' NIGHT OUT
or
WHAT'S THAT SILENCE
I HEAR?

There's an adult world out there waiting
to be discovered—a place where you eat
off real plates and where "preferred
seating" means a booth with a view
instead of a counter with saddle
seats and stirrups.

"Well, if you'd take me out more often, I wouldn't have
inadvertently ordered Lobster McNuggets!"

With today's fast-paced living it's easy for parents to forget what it's like to go out for a night on the town. We forget there's more to life than eating kiddie meals out of space saucers. There's an adult world out there waiting to be discovered—a place where you eat off real plates and where "preferred seating" means a booth with a view instead of a counter with saddle seats and stirrups.

It does exist, and sometimes we owe it to ourselves and to our families to get away from the McHustle-McBustle of life and find it.

I recall one particular evening when my husband decided it was time to do just that. He made reservations at one of the most expensive restaurants in our town. It was the type of establishment that didn't honor coupons or give out game tokens, and the only arches it had were in the maitre d's Gucci shoes. I couldn't wait.

We arrived at the restaurant about 15 minutes early for our 7:00 p.m. reservations and followed the valet parking arrows to the front entrance.

"Now, this is real class," I said in wide-eyed appraisal. "They're even going to park our car."

"Not ours," my husband said with a frown. "The valet appears to be waving us on."

"Why didn't you bring the good car?" I grumbled.

"This *is* the good car," he said as we stalled out trying to make it over a speed bump.

Once inside, we were able to relax and just enjoy the elegance, and there was plenty of it to enjoy. The menu didn't have pictures, the tablecloth didn't stick to our arms from dried catsup spills and the waiter didn't even know

111

what a booster seat was. In fact, he gagged when I inadvertently ordered chocolate milk.

"Look! They even give party hats," I exclaimed, pinning one to my hair.

"Those aren't party hats," my husband said, snatching it off my head. "They're our napkins. They fold them that way."

All in all, though, it was nice to get out and enjoy the finer side of life for a change, to be somewhere where we didn't have to eat out of Styrofoam or listen to little ones crying.

As a matter of fact, the only crying I did have to listen to was my husband's—when the check came.

25
HOW TO KEEP A SONG IN YOUR HEART—EVEN WHEN A FEW SOUR NOTES COME YOUR WAY

When you're driving down the freeway, 20 minutes late for Sunday School, try singing, "Hold the Fort for I Am Coming!"

"It's your heart. I don't know how to tell you this, but
we found a song in it!"

Life is so much easier when you go through it with a song in your heart. No matter what comes your way, you can usually find the perfect song to help get you through it.

For instance, when you're driving down the freeway, 20 minutes late for Sunday School, try singing, "Hold the Fort for I Am Coming!"

When you're hosting a birthday party for 30 rambunctious six-year-olds, humming "Blessed Quietness" just might help. And when they decide to turn it into a slumber party? Try "Hasten Thy Glorious Coming, Lord."

Your child's graduation? What better time for "It Took a Miracle"?

And when school lets out for the summer and you're faced with three long months of trying to entertain a houseful of adolescents, how about "Where Could I Go"?

When someone cuts in line in front of you at the bank, you might think about breaking into a few choruses of "I Shall Not Be Moved."

A traffic jam? Try singing "I'm Going Through."

A tax audit? How about "That Old Account Was Settled Long Ago"?

And when you rush to take the kids to school and run out of gas in your bathrobe and curlers, you might find comfort in that old favorite "Precious Hiding Place."

The important thing is just to keep a song in your heart. That way, even when a few sour notes do come your way, your walk with Him won't miss a beat.

Also Available from Regal Books

The Delicate Art of Dancing with Porcupines—Bob Phillips
Relating to prickly people is a lot like dancing with porcupines—difficult
to say the least. Family counselor Bob Phillips suggests that relating is a
delicate art that requires a knowledge of the four basic social styles.
Understand the reasons behind behavior—both your own and that of
others.   ISBN 0-8307-1333-6 5419749

We Didn't Know They Were Angels—Doris W. Greig
Discover that Christian hospitality really means "relaxed availability."
Hospitality isn't the same as entertaining and it doesn't need to be
intimidating. A warm heart, a friendly manner and a willing spirit is all you
need to be hospitable.   ISBN 0-8307-1335-2 5419750

**Bring Joy to a group of friends with the Joy of Living Bible Study
Series.** Take part in the joy of fellowship and Bible study with this
evangelical, non-denominational program for individual, church and
home study. Start with any one of the eight courses in this series.

Courage to Conquer: Studies in Daniel—Doris W. Greig
ISBN 0-8307-1285-2 5419489

Discovering God's Power: Studies in Genesis 1–17—Doris W. Greig
ISBN 0-8307-1361-1 5419845

Drinking from the Living Well: Studies in John 1–11—Doris W. Greig
ISBN 0-8307-1358-1 5419824

Exercising a Balanced Faith: Studies in James—Doris W. Greig
ISBN 0-8307-1310-7 5419649

Living in the Light: Studies in 1,2,3 John and Jude—Doris W. Greig
  ISBN 0-8307-1287-9 5419501

Power for Positive Living: Studies in Philippians and Colossians—
Doris W. Greig   ISBN 0-8307-1286-0 5419493

Walking in God's Way: Studies in Ruth and Esther—Ruth Bathauer
and Doris W. Greig   ISBN 0-8307-1284-4 5419474

Look for these and other Regal titles
at your local Christian bookstore.